March

Dear Jordan,

Our hope is that we
will share many more
Passover's together.

Love always,
Nanie + Grandpa

# מה נשתנה?

# Mah Nishtanah?

## הגדה של פסח לילדים
## A Passover Haggadah
## for Children

**Editor:** Shaul Meizlish

Adama Books   New York

**Graphic Artist:** A.I. Taub
**Graphic Production:** Studio Aesthetics
**Photography:** Ayalah Avidar
**English:**Shmuel Himelstein

**Adama Books, 306 West 38 Street, New York, NY 10018**

Printed in Israel

# INTRODUCTION

**Dear Parents,**

The Passover holiday (and especially the *Seder* night) is a holiday much beloved by all children, and the child plays a central role in it.

Not only is the child the object of the commandment incumbent on parents, "You shall tell it to your children," but he or she is involved in the preparations for the festival, such as helping to clean the home, searching for *Chametz* and then burning it, and at the *Seder* itself asking the "Four Questions" and "stealing" the *Afikoman*. By participating in the telling of the *Haggadah* story, the child is involved in the greatest national religious event that the Jews ever experienced, and begins to appreciate Judaism's eternal values.

This *Haggadah* is meant for all children, especially those that do not yet read fluently, and the very young .In order to make the *Haggadah* suitable for this age group, we have only printed the major portions of the *Haggadah*. For those unacquainted with Hebrew, we have supplied a transliteration of the Hebrew text using English letters.

To make the *Haggadah* most suitable for the young, we have arranged it so as to stress both the historical account and the various laws and customs involved with the *Seder* night. To make this a most meaningful volume for children, we have consulted with rabbis, psychologists and educators as to the type style, photographs and drawings. Somewhat older children can use this *Haggadah* together with the standard *Haggadah*.

Because of the age group to which this *Haggadah* is addressed, numerous liberties were taken in paraphrasing, rather than translating literally, the Hebrew text.

We would like to express special thanks to David and Yonah Rabinowitz of Ramat Gan, who opened their house to us, and to Mr. David Fogel of Pardes Chanah, who enlightened us with his magnificent collection of *Haggadot*.

We hope and pray that by means of this *Haggadah* our children will be able to relive the deliverance of our nation and its progress from slavery to freedom and independence, so that each child will feel as if he or she has just left Egypt, for the teling of this story is the major portion of the evening's commandment: "Even if we are all wise, and all know the Torah, we are still commanded to tell the story of the Exodus from Egypt."

A Happy and Kosher Passover!

S.M.

# SEARCHING FOR CHAMETZ

בְּדִיקַת חָמֵץ

Good Yomtov, children.
The night before the *Seder* night, daddy and the children look for *Chametz*, using a candle. Before we start looking for the *Chametz*, we say:

| | |
|---|---|
| **Baruch ata Adonay,** | <div dir="rtl">בָּרוּךְ אַתָּה יְיָ</div> |
| **Eloheinu melech ha'olam,** | <div dir="rtl">אֱלֹהֵינוּ מֶלֶךְ הָעוֹלָם</div> |
| **asher kideshanu** | <div dir="rtl">אֲשֶׁר קִדְּשָׁנוּ</div> |
| **be'mitzvotav vetzivanu** | <div dir="rtl">בְּמִצְוֹתָיו וְצִוָּנוּ</div> |
| **al bi'ur chametz.** | <div dir="rtl">עַל בִּעוּר חָמֵץ.</div> |

Blessed are you, God, king of the world, who told us to burn our *Chametz*.

The next day, we can only eat *Chametz* very early, up to nine o'clock. From nine o'clock, we can't eat *Chametz*, and can't even have any. All the *Chametz* we found last night must be burned in the morning. Just in case we missed some *Chametz* when we searched, we say that we don't want it to be ours. This is what we say:

| | |
|---|---|
| **Kol chamira vechamiya** | כָּל חֲמִירָא וַחֲמִיעָא |
| **de'ika bireshuti,** | דְּאִכָּא בִרְשׁוּתִי, |
| **de'chamitei u'delo** | דַּחֲמִתֵּיה וּדְלָא |
| **chamitei,** | חֲמִתֵּיה, |
| **de'bi'artei u'delo** | דִּבְעַרְתֵּיה וּדְלָא |
| **bi'artei, levateil,** | בְעַרְתֵּיה, לְבָטֵל, |
| **velehevi hefker** | וְלֶהֱוֵי הֶפְקֵר, |
| **ke'afra de'ara.** | כְּעַפְרָא דְאַרְעָא. |

# THE SEDER PLATE

סֵדֶר הַקְעָרָה

בֵּיצָה
Beitza

זְרוֹעַ
Zeroa

מָרוֹר
Maror

כַּרְפַּס
Karpas

חֲרֹסֶת
Charoset

חֲזֶרֶת
Chazeret

Three  Matzot          ג' מַצּוֹת

### What is the **Zeroa?**

This is a leg bone from a sheep or chicken, which mommy roasted. It reminds us of the *Zeroa Netuya* – God's hand that he stretched out to save the Jews in Egypt.

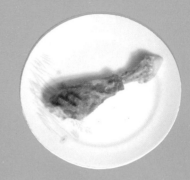

### What is the **Beitza?**

A roasted egg reminds us of a special sacrifice the Jews brought to the holy Temple in Jerusalem three times every year. *Pesach* was one of those times.

### What is **Maror?**

This is any vegetable which has a bitter taste, like lettuce or horseradish, and it reminds us how the Egyptians made the Jews' lives very bitter with their hard work.

## What is **Charoset?**

This is made of nuts, apples, dates, spices, raisins and wine. It reminds us of the cement the Jews used when they had to build buildings in Egypt.

## What is **Karpas?**

This is a raw or cooked vegetable, like a potato, carrot, parsley, radish or celery.

## What is **Chazeret?**

This is normally *Maror*, but grated. we eat *Chazeret* between two *Matzot*, to remind us of what Hillel used to do.

# LIGHTING THE CANDLES

הַדְלָקַת נֵרוֹת

Mommy and the girls in the family light the holiday candles and make this blessing:

| | |
|---|---|
| Baruch ata Adonay, | בָּרוּךְ אַתָּה יְיָ |
| Eloheinu melech ha'olam, | אֱלֹהֵינוּ מֶלֶךְ הָעוֹלָם |
| asher kideshanu | אֲשֶׁר קִדְּשָׁנוּ |
| be'mitzvotav vetzivanu | בְּמִצְוֹתָיו וְצִוָּנוּ |
| lehadlik ner shel Yomtov. | לְהַדְלִיק נֵר שֶׁל יוֹם טוֹב. |

Blessed are you, God, king of the world, who told us to light the holiday candles.

| | |
|---|---|
| Baruch ata Adonay, | בָּרוּךְ אַתָּה יְיָ |
| Eloheinu melech ha'olam, | אֱלֹהֵינוּ מֶלֶךְ הָעוֹלָם |
| shehecheyanu vekiyemanu | שֶׁהֶחֱיָנוּ וְקִיְּמָנוּ |
| vehigiyanu lazman hazeh. | וְהִגִּיעָנוּ לַזְּמַן הַזֶּה. |

Blessed are you, God, king of the world, who let us be here now.

# KADDESH  קַדֵּשׁ

How do we begin the holiday? We make *Kiddush* over wine.

On the *Seder* night we have to drink four cups of wine, because God used four different words to tell us how He saved us from Egypt. We pour the first cup of wine, and daddy says:

| | |
|---|---|
| **Baruch ata Adonay,** | בָּרוּךְ אַתָּה יְיָ |
| **Eloheinu melech ha'olam,** | אֱלֹהֵינוּ מֶלֶךְ הָעוֹלָם |
| **boreh pri hagafen.** | בּוֹרֵא פְּרִי הַגָּפֶן: |

Blessed are you, God, king of the world, who made wine.

| | |
|---|---|
| **Baruch ata Adonay,** | בָּרוּךְ אַתָּה יְיָ |
| **Eloheinu melech ha'olam,** | אֱלֹהֵינוּ מֶלֶךְ הָעוֹלָם |
| **asher  bachar banu mikol am** | אֲשֶׁר בָּחַר בָּנוּ מִכָּל עָם |
| **veromemanu mikol lashon** | וְרוֹמְמָנוּ מִכָּל לָשׁוֹן |
| **vekideshanu bemitzvotav.** | וְקִדְּשָׁנוּ בְּמִצְוֹתָיו. |
| **Vatiten lanu Adonay Eloheinu** | וַתִּתֶּן לָנוּ יְיָ אֱלֹהֵינוּ |
| **be'ahava mo'adim lesimcha,** | בְּאַהֲבָה מוֹעֲדִים לְשִׂמְחָה, |
| **chagim u'zmanim lesason, et** | חַגִּים וּזְמַנִּים לְשָׂשׂוֹן אֶת |
| **yom chag Ha'matzot hazeh,** | יוֹם חַג הַמַּצּוֹת הַזֶּה, |
| **z'man cheiruteinu mikra kodesh** | זְמַן חֵרוּתֵנוּ מִקְרָא קֹדֶשׁ |
| **zeicher liyetziyat mitzraim,** | זֵכֶר לִיצִיאַת מִצְרָיִם. |
| **ki vanu vacharta, ve'otanu** | כִּי בָנוּ בָחַרְתָּ וְאוֹתָנוּ |

| | |
|---|---|
| kidashta mikol ha'amim, | קִדַּשְׁתָּ מִכָּל הָעַמִּים, |
| u'mo'adei kodshecha besimcha | וּמוֹעֲדֵי קָדְשֶׁךָ בְּשִׂמְחָה |
| uvesason hinchaltanu. | וּבְשָׂשׂוֹן הִנְחַלְתָּנוּ. |
| Baruch ata Adonay, mekadeish | בָּרוּךְ אַתָּה יְיָ מְקַדֵּשׁ |
| yisrael vehaz'manim. | יִשְׂרָאֵל וְהַזְּמַנִּים. |

Blessed are you, God, king of the world, who chose us from all the other people, and made us holy. You love us and gave us our holidays to be happy, this *Pesach* day, the time when we became free. This reminds us of leaving Egypt. Blessed are you, God, king of the world, who made the Jews and our holidays holy.

We end with:

| | |
|---|---|
| Baruch ata Adonay, | בָּרוּךְ אַתָּה יְיָ |
| Eloheinu melech ha'olam, | אֱלֹהֵינוּ מֶלֶךְ הָעוֹלָם |
| shehecheyanu vekiyemanu | שֶׁהֶחֱיָנוּ וְקִיְּמָנוּ |
| vehigiyanu lazman hazeh. | וְהִגִּיעָנוּ לַזְּמַן הַזֶּה. |

Blessed are you, God, king of the world, who let us be here now.
Now we drink the first cup of wine.

# URECHATZ     וּרְחַץ

We wash our hands, but we don't say any
blessing *(Bracha)*.

# KARPAS     כַּרְפַּס

We take the vegetable we used for *Karpas* and dip it into salt water (water with salt in it). Then we say:

| | |
|---|---|
| **Baruch ata, Adonay,** | בָּרוּךְ אַתָּה יְיָ |
| **Eloheinu melech ha'olam,** | אֱלֹהֵינוּ מֶלֶךְ הָעוֹלָם |
| **borei p'ri ha'adama.** | בּוֹרֵא פְּרִי הָאֲדָמָה. |

Blessed are you, God, king of the world, who made vegetables.

# YACHATZ     יַחַץ

*Yachatz* means to break something. What do we break? Daddy breaks the middle *Matzah* into two pieces. He takes the bigger piece and puts it into a napkin. This is the *Afikoman*. What is the *Afikoman?* Wait, wait until the end of the meal...

# MAGID  מַגִּיד

Now we begin to tell the whole Pesach story.
God said that all daddies and mommies
should tell their children the story of how the
Jews left Egypt. This is a true story, that really
happened. A long time ago the Jews had to
work very hard in Egypt. Now we are free and
have our own country.

# Mah Nishtanah     מַה נִּשְׁתַּנָּה

| | |
|---|---|
| halayla hazeh mikol ha'laylot? Shebechol ha'laylot anu ochlin chametz u'matzah; halayla hazeh kulo matzah. | הַלַּיְלָה הַזֶּה מִכָּל הַלֵּילוֹת? שֶׁבְּכָל הַלֵּילוֹת אָנוּ אוֹכְלִין חָמֵץ וּמַצָּה. הַלַּיְלָה הַזֶּה כֻּלּוֹ מַצָּה. |

Why is this night different than any other night? Every other night we can eat bread and *Matzah*. Tonight we can only eat *Matzah*.

| | |
|---|---|
| Shebechol ha'laylot anu ochlim she'ar yerakot; halayla hazeh maror. | שֶׁבְּכָל הַלֵּילוֹת אָנוּ אוֹכְלִין שְׁאָר יְרָקוֹת. הַלַּיְלָה הַזֶּה מָרוֹר. |

Every other night we eat any vegetable we want to; tonight we have to eat the *Maror*, the bitter vegetable.

| | |
|---|---|
| Shebechol ha'laylot ein anu matbilin afilu pa'am echat; halayla hazeh, sh'tei fe'amim. | שֶׁבְּכָל הַלֵּילוֹת אֵין אָנוּ מַטְבִּילִין אֲפִילוּ פַּעַם אֶחָת. הַלַּיְלָה הַזֶּה שְׁתֵּי פְעָמִים. |

Every other night we don't dip anything; tonight we dip things two times – *Karpas* into water with salt, and *Maror* into *Charoset*.

| | |
|---|---|
| Shebechol ha'laylot anu ochlim bein yoshvin u'vain mesubin; halayla hazeh kulanu mesubin. | שֶׁבְּכָל הַלֵּילוֹת אָנוּ אוֹכְלִין בֵּין יוֹשְׁבִין וּבֵין מְסֻבִּין. הַלַּיְלָה הַזֶּה כֻּלָּנוּ מְסֻבִּין. |

Every other night we can lean if we want to; tonight we have to lean.

Daddy and the other people answer us:

Avadim hayinu        עֲבָדִים הָיִינוּ

lefar'oh be'mitzrayim,     לְפַרְעֹה בְּמִצְרָיִם.

vayotzi'einu Odanay     וַיּוֹצִיאֵנוּ יְיָ

Eloheinu misham       אֱלֹהֵינוּ מִשָּׁם

b'yad chazaka        בְּיָד חֲזָקָה

u'vi'zero'a netuya.      וּבִזְרוֹעַ נְטוּיָה.

We were slaves in Egypt. The Egyptians made us work very hard.
Then God took us out of Egypt.

# THE FOUR SONS

אַרְבָּעָה בָּנִים

**Keneged arba banim dibra Torah:**

כְּנֶגֶד אַרְבָּעָה בָּנִים דִּבְּרָה תּוֹרָה.

**eched chacham,** אֶחָד חָכָם,

**ve'echad rasha,** וְאֶחָד רָשָׁע,

**ve'echad tam,** וְאֶחָד תָּם,

**ve'echad she'eino yode'a lish'ol.** וְאֶחָד שֶׁאֵינוֹ יוֹדֵעַ לִשְׁאֹל.

The Torah mentions four kinds of sons.
One is clever. One is bad. One doesn't know a lot. One doesn't even know what to ask.

One is bad.

One doesn't know a lot.

One doesn't know what to ask.

One is clever.

Very many times the Jews had lots of troubles from other people, and God always helped and saved us. The whole family sings:

| | |
|---|---|
| Vihi she'amdah | וְהִיא שֶׁעָמְדָה |
| la'avoteinu velanu. | לַאֲבוֹתֵינוּ וְלָנוּ. |
| Shelo echad bilvad | שֶׁלֹּא אֶחָד בִּלְבַד |
| amad aleinu lechaloteinu. | עָמַד עָלֵינוּ לְכַלּוֹתֵנוּ. |
| Ela shebechol dor vador | אֶלָּא שֶׁבְּכָל דּוֹר וָדוֹר |
| omdim aleinu lechaloteinu, | עוֹמְדִים עָלֵינוּ לְכַלּוֹתֵנוּ, |
| veHakadosh Baruch Hu | וְהַקָּדוֹשׁ בָּרוּךְ הוּא |
| matzileinu miyadam. | מַצִּילֵנוּ מִיָּדָם. |

The same things that happened to our fathers happened to us. Every time there were bad people that wanted to hurt us, but God helped us.


We spill three drops of wine and say:

| | |
|---|---|
| Dam, va'eish, | דָּם וָאֵשׁ, |
| ve'timrot ashan. | וְתִימְרוֹת עָשָׁן. |

Blood, fire and thick smoke.
These were some of the miracles God did for us in Egypt.

# THE TEN PLAGUES

# עֶשֶׂר מַכּוֹת

Eilu eser makot sheheivi
Hakadosh Baruch Hu
al hamitzrim be'mitzrayim,
ve'eilu hein:

אֵלּוּ עֶשֶׂר מַכּוֹת שֶׁהֵבִיא
הַקָּדוֹשׁ בָּרוּךְ הוּא
עַל הַמִּצְרִים בְּמִצְרַיִם.
וְאֵלּוּ הֵן:

God punished Egypt with ten plagues. These are the plagues:

We spill a little bit of wine whenever we mention a plague. We say the ten plagues together.

דָּם

**Dam**

blood

**צְפַרְדֵּעַ**

**Tzefardeya**

frogs

**כִּנִּים**

**Kinim**

lice

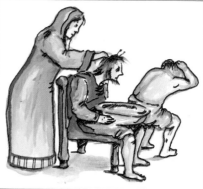

**עָרוֹב**

**Arov**

wild animals

# דֶּבֶר
**Dever**

sickness

# שְׁחִין
**Shechin**

blisters

# בָּרָד
**Barad**

hail

**אַרְבֶּה**

**Arbeh**

locusts

**חֹשֶׁךְ**

**Choshech**

darkness

**מַכַּת בְּכוֹרוֹת**

**Makat bechorot**

killing the
Egyptian
oldest children.

## Kama ma'alot tovot lamakom aleinu:
כַּמָּה מַעֲלוֹת טוֹבוֹת לַמָּקוֹם עָלֵינוּ

God did so many good things for us:

**Ilu hotziyanu**
**mimitzrayim velo**
**asa bahem shefatim,**
**dayenu.**

אִלּוּ הוֹצִיאָנוּ
מִמִּצְרַיִם וְלֹא
עָשָׂה בָהֶם שְׁפָטִים,
דַּיֵּנוּ.

If God took us out of Egypt and didn't punish the Egyptians for being bad to us, that would be enough.

**Ilu kara lanu**
**et hayam**
**velo he'eviranu**
**betocho becharava,**
**dayenu.**

אִלּוּ קָרַע לָנוּ
אֶת הַיָּם
וְלֹא הֶעֱבִירָנוּ
בְּתוֹכוֹ בֶּחָרָבָה,
דַּיֵּנוּ.

If God split the sea for us, but didn't let us go through it without getting wet, that would be enough.

**Ilu hichnisanu**
**le'eretz yisrael**
**velo bana lanu**
**et beit habechira,**
**dayenu.**

אִלּוּ הִכְנִיסָנוּ
לְאֶרֶץ יִשְׂרָאֵל,
וְלֹא בָנָה לָנוּ
אֶת בֵּית הַבְּחִירָה,
דַּיֵּנוּ.

If God brought us into Israel, but didn't build the holy Temple, it would be enough.

We have to talk about three important things at the *Seder:* about the sacrifice that was bought on *Pesach* a long time ago, about the *Matzah,* and about the *Maror.*

# PESACH, MATZAH U'MAROR

# פֶּסַח מַצָּה וּמָרוֹר

| | |
|---|---|
| Pesach | פֶּסַח |
| shehayu avoteinu ochlim | שֶׁהָיוּ אֲבוֹתֵינוּ אוֹכְלִים |
| biz'man shebeit hamikdash | בִּזְמַן שֶׁבֵּית הַמִּקְדָּשׁ |
| haya kayam, al shum ma? | הָיָה קַיָּם, עַל שׁוּם מָה? |
| Al shum shepsach | עַל שׁוּם שֶׁפָּסַח |
| Hakadosh Baruch Hu | הַקָּדוֹשׁ בָּרוּךְ הוּא |
| al batei avoteinu | עַל בָּתֵּי אֲבוֹתֵינוּ |
| bemitzrayim. | בְּמִצְרָיִם. |

Why did the Jews eat the *Pesach* sacrifice when we had the Temple in Jerusalem? That was to remind them how God skipped the homes of the Jews when he punished the Egyptians and killed all their oldest children.
*Pesach* in Hebrew means to skip.

Matzah
zu she'anu ochlim,
al shum ma?
Al shum shelo hispik
batzeikam shel avoteinu
lehachmitz.

מַצָּה
זוֹ שֶׁאָנוּ אוֹכְלִים,
עַל שׁוּם מַה?
עַל שׁוּם שֶׁלֹּא הִסְפִּיק
בְּצֵקָם שֶׁל אֲבוֹתֵינוּ
לְהַחְמִיץ.

Why do we eat *Matzah?* The reason is that when the Jews left Egypt, they had to rush out very fast, and they had to bake their bread before it had a chance to get big and fluffy, like the bread we eat. We see that the Jews trusted God so much, that they didn't even try to prepare food for their long trip.

That is why we eat *Matzah* at the *Seder.*

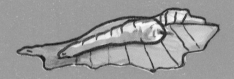

| Maror | מָרוֹר |
|---|---|
| ze she'anu ochlim, | זֶה שֶׁאָנוּ אוֹכְלִים |
| al shum ma? | עַל שׁוּם מָה? |
| Al shum | עַל שׁוּם |
| shemareru hamitzrim | שֶׁמֵּרְרוּ הַמִּצְרִים |
| et chaye avoteinu | אֶת חַיֵּי אֲבוֹתֵינוּ |
| bemitzrayim. | בְּמִצְרָיִם. |

Why do we eat *Maror* at the *Seder?* This is to remind us how the Egyptians made the lives of the Jews bitter because of all the hard work. When we eat the *Maror,* we remember how hard the Jews had to work in Egypt.

We drink the second cup of wine and say:

Baruch ata Adonay,
Eloheinu melech
ha'olam,
borei pri hagafen.

בָּרוּךְ אַתָּה יְיָ,
אֱלֹהֵינוּ מֶלֶךְ
הָעוֹלָם
בּוֹרֵא פְּרִי הַגָּפֶן.

Blessed are you, God, king of the world, who made wine.

# ROCHTZA רָחְצָה

We wash our hands, but this time we do say a blessing:

Baruch ata Adonay,
Eloheinu melech ha'olam,
asher kideshanu
be'mitzvotav vetzivanu
al netilat yadayim.

בָּרוּךְ אַתָּה יְיָ,
אֱלֹהֵינוּ מֶלֶךְ הָעוֹלָם
אֲשֶׁר קִדְּשָׁנוּ
בְּמִצְוֹתָיו, וְצִוָּנוּ
עַל נְטִילַת יָדָיִם.

Blessed are you, God, king of the world, who told us to wash our hands.

46

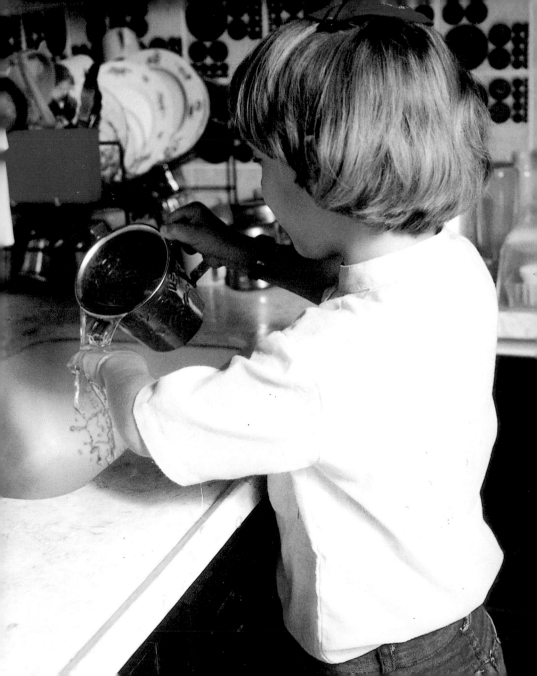

# MOTZI    מוֹצִיא

Daddy takes the three *Matzot* and says:

**Baruch ata Adonay,**      בָּרוּךְ אַתָּה יְיָ,
**Eloheinu melech ha'olam,**    אֱלֹהֵינוּ מֶלֶךְ הָעוֹלָם
**hamotzi lechem**      הַמוֹצִיא לֶחֶם
**min ha'aretz.**      מִן הָאָרֶץ.

Blessed are you, God, king of the world, who made bread from the earth.


# MATZAH    מַצָה

Daddy puts down the bottom *Matzah,* and
then says:

**Baruch ata Adonay,**      בָּרוּךְ אַתָּה יְיָ,
**Eloheinu melech ha'olam,**    אֱלֹהֵינוּ מֶלֶךְ הָעוֹלָם
**asher kideshanu**      אֲשֶׁר קִדְּשָׁנוּ
**be'mitzvotav vetzivanu**    בְּמִצְוֹתָיו, וְצִוָּנוּ
**al achilat matzah.**      עַל אֲכִילַת מַצָה.

Blessed are you, God, king of the world, who told us to eat *Matzah*.

Now daddy gives everybody a piece of *Matzah*
to eat.

# MAROR מָרוֹר

We take the *Maror* and dip it into *Charoset*,
then we say:


**Baruch ata Adonay,** בָּרוּךְ אַתָּה יְיָ,

**Eloheinu melech ha'olam,** אֱלֹהֵינוּ מֶלֶךְ הָעוֹלָם,

**asher kideshanu** אֲשֶׁר קִדְּשָׁנוּ

**be'mitzvotav vetzivanu** בְּמִצְוֹתָיו וְצִוָּנוּ

**al achilat maror.** עַל אֲכִילַת מָרוֹר.

Blessed are you, God, king of the world, who told us to eat *Maror*.


Now we eat the *Maror*.

# KORECH　　כּוֹרֵךְ

Hillel made the first sandwich. He took the bottom *Matzah,* put some *Maror* on it, and ate both together. He did it this way, because the Torah tells us to eat "with *Matzah* and *Maror.*"

# SHULCHAN ORECH　　שֻׁלְחָן עוֹרֵךְ

Now we begin to eat our meal. First we eat some hard-boiled eggs in salt water, to remind us how the Jews crossed the Red Sea. Sea water is very salty.

Why do we use a hard-boiled egg? The egg is like the Jews in one way. The more you cook an egg, the harder it gets. If Jews have troubles, they get more strong.

# SOME NAMES OF THE HOLIDAY שְׁמוֹת הֶחָג

During the meal, daddy asked everybody how many names there are for this holiday. These are the names.

**Pesach** — This reminds us how God skipped the houses of the Jews and punished the bad Egyptians.

**Chag Hamatzot** — We also call it the "holiday of *Matzot*," because the Jews left Egypt in such a hurry that they could only take *Matzot* and not bread.

**Chag Hacheirut** — It is also called the "holiday of our freedom." For many, many years the Jews had to work for the Egyptians until God saved them and made them free.

**Chag Ha'aviv —** Another name is the "holiday of the spring season," because the Jews became free in the spring-time.

# GOLD OR FIRE?    זָהָב אוֹ אֵשׁ

During the meal, daddy tells us stories about the time that the Jews were in Egypt. Why did Moses stutter when he spoke? When Moses was very small, the Egyptian officers wanted to know whether they should let him live or throw him into the river, just like they did with the other little Jewish boys. They decided to see if he was smart or not. If he was smart they would throw him into the river, and if he wasn't they would let him live. What was their test? They took two plates. One of them had some very hot coals, and the other had some very shiny gold. If he would take the gold they would know he was smart, and then they would kill him. If he took the coals, they would leave him alive.

Moses wanted to take the gold, but an angel pushed his hand away to the other plate, and he took the burning hot coals. When he burned his hand, he put his fingers into his mouth, and that burned his tongue. That was why Moses stuttered.

# TZAFUN     צָפוּן

Are you tired? Wait a little bit longer. Soon a surprise will wake you up. It is *Afikoman* time! After the meal we have to find the *Afikoman* that daddy hid, and we eat it before thanking God for our food.

What does the word *Afikoman* mean? It comes from a language called Aramaic, and is really made up of two words: *Afiko – Kaman*. This means "take it away from me." After we eat the *Afikoman*, we are not allowed to eat anything else that night, and we are saying "take away all the other food·from me."

The *Afikoman* is the half piece of *Matzah* daddy put away before. It reminds us that long ago, when all the Jews lived in Israel, they would come to the Temple in Jerusalem and eat a special *Pesach* sacrifice there.

Now that you found the *Afikoman*, you can ask for a present. Until you give back the *Afikoman* to daddy, the *Seder* can't go on.

# BARECH

בָּרֵךְ

After we eat the *Afikoman,* we pour the third cup of wine, and thank God for our meal:

| | |
|---|---|
| Baruch ata Adonay, Eloheinu | בָּרוּךְ אַתָּה יְיָ, אֱלֹהֵינוּ |
| melech ha'aolam, hazan et | מֶלֶךְ הָעוֹלָם, הַזָּן אֶת |
| ha'olam kulo betuvo, be'chein, | הָעוֹלָם כֻּלּוֹ בְּטוּבוֹ, בְּחֵן |
| be'chesed uve'rachamim. | בְּחֶסֶד וּבְרַחֲמִים, |
| Hu notein lechem lechol basar | הוּא נוֹתֵן לֶחֶם לְכָל בָּשָׂר, |
| ki le'olam chasdo, uvetuvo | כִּי לְעוֹלָם חַסְדּוֹ. וּבְטוּבוֹ |
| hagadol tamid lo chasar lanu, | הַגָּדוֹל תָּמִיד לֹא חָסַר לָנוּ, |
| ve'al yechsar lanu, mazon | וְאַל יֶחְסַר לָנוּ מָזוֹן |
| le'olam va'ed, ba'avur shemo | לְעוֹלָם וָעֶד. בַּעֲבוּר שְׁמוֹ |
| hagadol. Ki hu eil zan | הַגָּדוֹל, כִּי הוּא אֵל זָן |
| umefarnes lakol, umeitiv lakol, | וּמְפַרְנֵס לַכֹּל, וּמֵטִיב לַכֹּל, |
| u'meichin mazon lechol | וּמֵכִין מָזוֹן לְכָל |
| beriyotav asher bara. Ka'amur, | בְּרִיּוֹתָיו אֲשֶׁר בָּרָא. כָּאָמוּר: |
| poteiyach et yadecha u'masbia | פּוֹתֵחַ אֶת יָדֶךָ וּמַשְׂבִּיעַ |
| lechol chai ratzon. Baruch ata | לְכָל חַי רָצוֹן. בָּרוּךְ אַתָּה |
| Adonay, hazan et hakol. | יְיָ, הַזָּן אֶת הַכֹּל. |

We thank you, God, king of the world, who gives everyone in the world food. God gives everyone bread, because He is kind to all. He is very good. He always gave us food. and wil always give it to us. Blessed are you, God, who gives everyone food.

\* \* \*

Uve'nei yerushalayim
ir hakodesh bimeheira
beyameinu, baruch ata
Adonay, bonei berachamav
yerushalayim, amein.

וּבְנֵה יְרוּשָׁלַיִם
עִיר הַקֹּדֶשׁ בִּמְהֵרָה
בְיָמֵינוּ: בָּרוּךְ אַתָּה
יְיָ, בּוֹנֵה בְרַחֲמָיו
יְרוּשָׁלָיִם. אָמֵן.

Please build Jerusalem soon. Blessed are you, God, who builds Jerusalem. Amen.

★ ★ ★

Harachaman, hu yizakeinu limot hamashiach ulechayei
ha'olam haba.
Harachaman hu yanchileinu
yom shekulo tov.

הָרַחֲמָן, הוּא יְזַכֵּנוּ לִימוֹת הַמָּשִׁיחַ וּלְחַיֵּי הָעוֹלָם הַבָּא.
הָרַחֲמָן, הוּא יַנְחִילֵנוּ
יוֹם שֶׁכֻּלּוֹ טוֹב,

God will bring us the *Mashiach*, who will save us and let us live in *Olam Haba*. God will make a time for us when everything will be good.

מִגְדּוֹל יְשׁוּעוֹת מַלְכּוֹ, וְעוֹשֶׂה חֶסֶד לִמְשִׁיחוֹ, לְדָוִד וּלְזַרְעוֹ עַד עוֹלָם: עֹשֶׂה שָׁלוֹם בִּמְרוֹמָיו, הוּא יַעֲשֶׂה שָׁלוֹם עָלֵינוּ וְעַל כָּל יִשְׂרָאֵל וְאִמְרוּ אָמֵן.

Migdol yeshu'ot malko, ve'oseh chesed limeshicho,
le'david ule'zar'o ad olam. Oseh shalom bimeromav, hu
ya'aseh shalom aleinu, ve'al kol yisrael, ve'imru amein.

God will help our king and our *Mashiach*, who will come from David's children. God who makes peace in heaven should also make peace in the world. Amen.

## We now drink the third cup, and say:

**Baruch ata Adonay,**
**Eloheinu melech ha'olam,**
**borei pri hagafen.**

בָּרוּךְ אַתָּה יְיָ,
אֱלֹהֵינוּ מֶלֶךְ הָעוֹלָם,
בּוֹרֵא פְּרִי הַגָּפֶן.

Blessed are you, God, king of the world, who made wine.

# THE CUP
# OF ELIJAH

כּוֹסוֹ שֶׁל
אֵלִיָּהוּ

Now is the time of the cup of the prophet
Elijah.
We pour a special cup of wine for him, then
we open our front door and say:

| | |
|---|---|
| **Shefoch chametecha al** | שְׁפֹךְ חֲמָתְךָ אֶל |
| **hagoyim asher lo yeda'ucha** | הַגּוֹיִם אֲשֶׁר לֹא יְדָעוּךָ, |
| **ve'al hamamlachot asher** | וְעַל מַמְלָכוֹת אֲשֶׁר |
| **beshimecha lo kar'a'u:** | בְּשִׁמְךָ לֹא קָרָאוּ: |
| **Ki achal et ya'akov,** | כִּי אָכַל אֶת יַעֲקֹב, |
| **ve'et naveihu heishamu:** | וְאֶת נָוֵהוּ הֵשַׁמּוּ: |
| **Shefoch aleihem za'amecha** | שְׁפֹךְ עֲלֵיהֶם זַעְמֶךָ |
| **ve'charon apecha yasigeim:** | וַחֲרוֹן אַפְּךָ יַשִּׂיגֵם: |
| **Tirdof be'af vetashmideim** | תִּרְדֹּף בְּאַף וְתַשְׁמִידֵם |
| **mi'tachat shemei Adonay.** | מִתַּחַת שְׁמֵי יְיָ. |

God, punish the people who don't listen to you, and who are bad to the
Jews.

# HALEL     הַלֵּל

We pour the fourth cup of wine, and we say
the last part of the *Halel* prayer, praising God.

| | |
|---|---|
| **Yisrael, betach ba'donay,** | יִשְׂרָאֵל בְּטַח בַּיְיָ. |
| **ezram u'maginam hu.** | עֶזְרָם וּמָגִנָּם הוּא: |
| **Beit Aharon betach ba'donay,** | בֵּית אַהֲרֹן בִּטְחוּ בַיְיָ. |
| **ezram u'maginam hu.** | עֶזְרָם וּמָגִנָּם הוּא: |
| **Yirei Adonay bitechu ba'donay,** | יִרְאֵי יְיָ בִּטְחוּ בַיְיָ. |
| **ezram u'maginam hu.** | עֶזְרָם וּמָגִנָּם הוּא: |

Jews, trust God, because he helps us.
Children of Aaron, trust God, because he helps us.

| | |
|---|---|
| **Odecha ki initani,** | אוֹדְךָ כִּי עֲנִיתָנִי, |
| **vatehi li li'shu'a.** | וַתְּהִי לִי לִישׁוּעָה. |
| **Even ma'asu habonim,** | אֶבֶן מָאֲסוּ הַבּוֹנִים, |
| **hayeta lerosh pinah.** | הָיְתָה לְרֹאשׁ פִּנָּה. |
| **Mei'eit Adonay hayeta zot,** | מֵאֵת יְיָ הָיְתָה זֹּאת, |
| **hi nifle'at be'eineinu.** | הִיא נִפְלָאת בְּעֵינֵינוּ. |
| **Zeh hayom asa Adonay,** | זֶה הַיּוֹם עָשָׂה יְיָ, |
| **nagila venismecha bo.** | נָגִילָה וְנִשְׂמְחָה בוֹ. |

I thank God, because you answered me and helped me.
The stone that nobody wanted became the most important one.
God did this, it was wonderful.
This is the day God made, we will be happy on it.

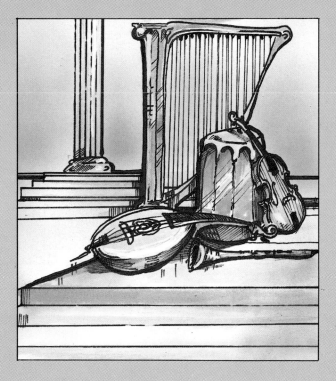

At the end of the *Seder,* we drink the fourth cup of wine. We say:

**Baruch ata Adonay,**
**Eloheinu melech ha'olam,**
**borei pri hagafen.**

בָּרוּךְ אַתָּה יְיָ,
אֱלֹהֵינוּ מֶלֶךְ הָעוֹלָם,
בּוֹרֵא פְּרִי הַגָּפֶן.

Blessed are you, God, king of the world, who made wine.

Here is whree the *Haggadah* actually ends.

חֲסַל סִדּוּר פֶּסַח כְּהִלְכָתוֹ.

**Chasal sidur pesach ke-hilcato.**

# LESHANAH HABA-AH BI-YERUSHALAYIM HA- BENUYAH.

לְשָׁנָה הַבָּאָה
בִּירוּשָׁלַיִם הַבְּנוּיָה.

But how can we leave the **Seder** table without singing the beautiful *Seder* songs?
We all shall sing:

# ECHAD, MI'YODE'A

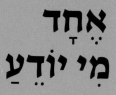

אֶחָד
מִי יוֹדֵעַ

Echad, mi yode'a?
Echad ani yode'a. Echad
Eloheinu she'bashamayim
uva'aretz.

Shnayim, mi yode'a?
Shnayim ani yode'a. Shnei
luchot habrit, echad
Eloheinu she'bashamayim
uva'aretz.

Shlosha mi yode'a?
Shlosha ani yode'a. Shlosha
avot, shnei luchot habrit,
echad Eloheinu
she'bashamayim uva'aretz.

Arba mi yode'a?
Arba ani yode'a. Arba
imahot, shlosha avot, shnei
luchot habrit, echad
Eloheinu she'bashamayim
uva'aretz.

Chamisha mi yode'a?
Chamisha ani yode'a.
Hamisha chumshai torah,
arba imahot, shlosha avot,

shnei luchot habrit, echad
Eloheinu she'bashamayim
uva'aretz.

Shisha mi yode'a?
Shisha ani yod'ea. Shisha
sidrei mishna, chamisha
chumshei torah, arba
imahot, shlosha avot, shnei
luchot habrit, echad
Eloheinu she'bashamayim
uva'aretz.

Shiva mi yode'a?
Shiva ani yode'a. Shiva
yemei shabta, shisha sidrei
mishna, chamisha chumshei
torah, arba imahot, shlosha
avot, shnei luchot habrit,
echad Eloheinu
she'bashamayim uva'aretz.

Shmona mi yode'a?
Shmona ani yode'a. Shmona
yemei mila, shiva yemei
shabta, shisha sidrei mishna,
chamisha chumshei torah,
arba imahot, shlosha avot,
shnei luchot habrit, echad
Eloheinu she'bashamayim
uva'aretz.

# ECHAD ELOHEINU SHE'BASHAMAYIM UVA'ARETZ

אֶחָד אֱלֹהֵינוּ
שֶׁבַּשָּׁמַיִם וּבָאָרֶץ

# CHAD GADYA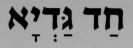

Chad gadya, chad gadya,
dezabin aba bi'trei zuzei,
chad gadya, chad gadya.

Ve'ata shunra ve'achla
legadya dezabin aba bi'trei
zuzei, chad gadya, chad
gadya.

Ve'ata kalba ve'nashach
leshunra, de'achla legadya,
dezabin aba bi'trei zuzei,
chad gadya, chad gadya.

Ve'ata chutra ve'hika
lekalba, de nashach leshunra,
de'achla legadya,
dezabin aba bi'trei zuzei,
chad gadya, chad gadya.

Ve'ata nura ve'saraf lechutra
dehika lekalba, denashach
leshunra, de'achla legadya,
dezabin aba bi'trei zuzei,
chad gadya, chad gadya.

Ve'ata maya ve'chaba
lenura, desasraf lechutra,
dehika lekalba, denashach
leshunra, de'achala legadya,
dezabin aba bi'trei zuzei,
chad gadya, chad gadya.

Ve'ata tora ve'shata lemaya,
dechaba lenura, desaraf
lechutra, dehika lekalba,
denashach leshunra, de'achla
legadya, dezabin aba bi'trei
zuzei, chad gadya, chad
gadya.

Ve'ata ha'shochet ve'shachat
letora, deshata lemaya,
dechaba lenura, desaraf
lechutra, dehika lekalba,
denashach leshunra,
de'achala legadya, dezabin
aba bitrei zuzei, chad gadya,
chad gadya.

Ve'ata malach hamavet
ve'shachat leshochet,
deshachat letora, deshata
lemaya, dechaba lenura,
desaraf lechutra,
dehika lekalba,
denashach leshunra, de'achla
legadya, dezabin aba bi'trei
zuzei, chad gadya, chad
gadya.

Ve'ata Hakadosh Baruch Hu
ve'shachat le'malach
hamavet, deshachat
leshochet, deshachat letora,
deshata lemaya, dechaba
lenura, desaraf
lechutra, dehika lekalba,
denashach leshunra,
de'achla legadya, dezabin
aba bi'trei zuzei, chad gadya,
chad gadya.

One kid, one kid, that daddy bought for two *Zuzim*, one kid, one kid.
And a cat came, and ate the kid.
And a dog came, and bit the cat.
And a stick came, and beat the dog.
And a fire came, and burned the stick.
And a water came, and put out the fire.
And an ox came, and drank tne water.
And the *Shochet* came, and killed the ox.
And the Angel of Death came, and killed the *Shochet*.
And God came, and killed the Angel of Death, that killed the *Shochet*,
that killed the ox, that drank the water, that put out the fire, that
burned the stick, that hit the dog, that bit the cat, that ate the kid. One
kid, one kid.